Euphorbias

Don Witton

Introduction

Euphorbias: Some Facts and Figures
 History
 Geography
 Botany

Euphorbias in the Garden
 Cultivation
 Pests & Diseases
 Plant Associations
 Cut Flowers

Propagation
 Seed
 Cuttings
 Division

An Alphabetical Listing

Where to see Euphorbias

Where to buy Euphorbias

Some Helpful Lists

The Euphorbia Year

References

Front cover: *Euphorbia donii*

All drawings, including the front cover, by Cyril Stocks
Edited and typeset by George Parker
Consultant editor to the Booklet Series: Tony Lord

© The Hardy Plant Society – July 2000

ISBN 0 901687 16 2

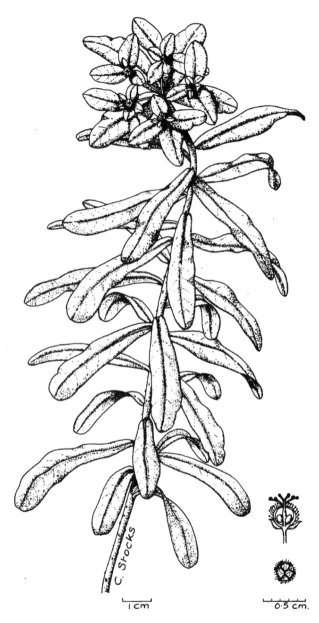

1 cm

0·5 cm.

Euphorbia polychroma

2

Acknowledgements

I HOPE THAT THIS BOOKLET will be found helpful and informative by those gardeners, both novice and experienced, who are lovers of euphorbias. Although I have thoroughly enjoyed writing it, the finished article would not have been possible without the help of a number of people.

Roger Turner, the author of *Euphorbias - A Gardener's Guide*, has given much help and friendly advice. Gary Dunlop, holder of a National Collection of euphorbias in Northern Ireland has also provided much information on cultivation and varieties. Lesley Witton, Head of English at Manchester High School for Girls, eradicated the grammatical errors in my script.

The following people have also helped with information on cultivars, cultivation and propagation: Judith Bradshaw, Catforth Gardens; Bob Brown, Cotswold Garden Flowers; Billy Carruthers, Binny Plants; J. M. Gardiner, Curator, RHS Garden, Wisley; Sally Gregson, Mill Cottage Plants; Christine Liddle, Birkheads Cottage Garden Nursery; Paul O'Carroll, Pandora Nursery; Timothy Walker, Oxford Botanic Garden; Charis Ward, Abbey Dore Court Garden; David Ward, Manager, Beth Chatto Nursery; Michael Wickenden, Cally Gardens.

Cyril Stocks, a fellow member of the Nottingham & Derby NCCPG, has produced the line drawings.

To all these kind and busy people I offer my grateful thanks. I cannot leave this page without mentioning my wife, Dot, for tolerating and understanding my passion for herbaceous perennials in general and euphorbias in particular; for all the hours spent without complaint with an absentee husband - thank you.

Introduction

GREENY YELLOWY FLOWERS; sap that can irritate and blister skin; some species with borderline hardiness, whilst others propagate themselves rather too vigorously; and then there's the problem of mildew - on the face of it, garden euphorbias don't appear to have very much going for them. Yet there are twelve different euphorbias that have been given the Royal Horticultural Society's Award of Garden Merit and many others that are becoming very popular with garden designers, keen plantsmen and gardeners. So what is it about spurges that makes them desirable garden plants?

To start with, they are first class foliage plants and, as many species are evergreen, the handsome clean cut lines of the leaves add stature to any garden scene - whether it be on the shortest or the longest day of the year. Euphorbias exhibit a wonderful variety of leaf shape, size and colour. For example, the robust leathery dark green leaves of *E. amygdaloides* var. *robbiae* contrast greatly with the small feathery purple foliage of *E. cyparissias* 'Fens Ruby'. The blue-grey sharply-pointed leaves of *E. rigida* would be hard to place visually in the same genus as the deep-maroon rounded leaves of *E. dulcis* 'Chameleon'. There are also numerous variegated forms such as *E. polychroma* 'Lacy' and *E. characias* subsp. *wulfenii* 'Emmer Green' .

Green flowers? The main floral colour is undoubtedly an addictive lime shade of yellow, but they can also be red (*E. griffithii* 'Fireglow'), orange (*E. g.* 'King's Caple'), white (*E. marginata*), gold (*E. characias* subsp. *wulfenii* 'Lambrook Gold') and pale lemon (*E. characias* subsp. *wulfenii* 'Bosahan'). The main flowering time is late winter and early spring. At a time when hellebores are going over and most other herbaceous perennials are just awakening from their winter dormancy, euphorbias demand centre stage in the garden, almost single handedly. They provide height, form, hot vibrant colours, and are a spectacular sight from March to May. They will then step away from the limelight during the summer but still provide a backdrop of foliage in the garden bed. Having said that, there are numerous lesser-known species - but nevertheless very good garden plants - which will prolong the unique chartreuse display throughout the summer and into the autumn.

Caustic sap? The question of the milky white sap or latex needs to be approached with common sense. Wear gloves and take care if you have sensitive skin. If sap does come into contact with your skin, I have found the best way to remove it is with neat washing up liquid. On the positive side, very few garden pests seem to bother euphorbias.

Borderline hardiness? Good cultivation, drainage and a sheltered position helps to protect any garden plant. Euphorbias are no exception to this rule. Also, many euphorbias are hardier than some people think. Take *E. mellifera* for instance. Some books state that it is dubiously hardy and will not survive outside north of Birmingham. The writer has heard of it taking -13°C and being none the worse for its experience. This plant hails from the Canary Islands where these temperatures would not be encountered. Here in Sheffield it thrives and is a very handsome 1.2m (4ft) plant. Today's mild British winters are also enabling gardeners to grow some of the more tender euphorbias more successfully, as cold snaps are not as severe or as long as they were twenty years ago.

Prolific propagation? This should not be a problem with strategic siting of plants and good garden husbandry. Runners like *E. cyparissias* would prove disastrous planted in a prize rockery. Far better to grow it in a pot or a wild area or as ground cover amongst tough shrubs. Any unwanted runners can be pulled out in spring. Species that seed freely need to be deadheaded before dropping their seed and any stray seedlings hoed out in spring. These should be normal garden tasks performed on a regular basis in any gardener's calendar.

Mildew? People who complain about mildew on euphorbias usually grow the two or three commonest varieties that are always available at the garden centres in spring. There are many, many species which are unaffected by mildew; gardeners who do not like mildew would do well to stick with these. Fortunately, the few species that contract mildew do so in the main after the flowering period is over and it does not detract from the floral display.

So, despite the apparent drawbacks mentioned initially, once one starts to delve a little deeper into the euphorbia family - and if foliage and form are high on one's list of priorities - there will be found a quite remarkable botanical family and many top class garden plants.

Euphorbias: Some Facts & Figures

HISTORY

Euphorbias have been grown and recorded since Ancient Greek times. However, the three spurges first mentioned by Greek writers (Paralios, Myrtites and Characias) were called 'Tithymalus'. The name 'euphorbia' was probably first used in Roman times, and it is said that King Juba of Mauretania discovered a plant and named it after his physician Euphorbus. This plant was one of the succulent euphorbias of Morocco.

Subsequent herbaceous euphorbias were all classified under the tithymalus name with the succulent euphorbias considered a separate genus. The first person to make a botanical link between euphorbia and tithymalus was Andrea Cesalpino in 1583, and in 1753 Linnaeus listed both groups of plants under the one euphorbia banner. There they have remained until the present time, when there are now known to be around 2000 species.

The English common name of spurge comes from the Latin word *expurgare*, meaning to purge out, which refers to the times in history when the sap was used medicinally as a cure for a variety of ills (without a great deal of success I would think, possibly even making the patient worse!)

GEOGRAPHY

Encapsulated within the 2000 or so species one will find almost every kind of plant. As well as herbaceous perennials and succulents there are hardy annuals (*E. peplus* is a common garden weed), biennials (*E. lathyris* the unusual caper spurge), and tender shrubs (*E. pulcherrima* is a tender deciduous 1.75m (5½ft) shrub from Mexico better known and grown as the house plant, poinsettia). Trees and cacti-like plants also make an appearance. As befits one of the six largest genera of flowering plants, the geographical distribution of the genus is on a world-wide scale and they can be found growing in just about every corner of the planet. Many are weedy annuals whilst the vast majority of euphorbia species come from tropical and sub-tropical climates and are unsuitable for outdoor cultivation in Britain.

Of the herbaceous perennial species with which this book is mainly concerned, there are about 80 species so far introduced that can be

Showing areas where euphorbias originate

grown outside in Britain. They originate mainly from Europe or temperate Asia. This is a relatively small band across the world (see map on page 7). Its perimeter stretches from China in the east (*E. pekinensis*) to the Azores in the west (*E. stygiana*). The northern limit is southern Scandinavia (*E. palustris*) whilst *E. nereidum* can be found in Morocco, North Africa. Euphorbias that grow near the warmer peripherals of this band will obviously find life difficult in exposed northern British gardens so shelter and protection may be needed to keep the plants happy. Within this band, euphorbias can be found growing in most habitats from the sandy coasts of Europe (*E. paralias*) to the high mountain slopes of the Himalaya (*E. wallichii* is found as high as 4000m (13000 ft). *E. palustris* grows in wet marshy land and beside streams and ponds, whilst there are many grey leaved species such as *E. rigida* that revel in a hot sunny aspect with stony, free draining soil. Contrast these with the British native wood spurge *E. amygdaloides* that prefers dappled shade and a richer soil.

BOTANY

Most of the euphorbias described in this book are multi-stemmed, leafy herbaceous perennials. The exceptions are one or two annuals and biennials; *E. spinosa* and *E. acanthothamnos* are dwarf shrubs and *E. mellifera* and *E. stygiana* are trees in their natural habitat but behave like other evergreen perennials in the British climate.

The roots of most species are clump forming, although *E. characias* has a taproot whilst others produce underground runners and spread. In some species, the spread is slow enough so as not to pose a problem while others can be rampant sprinters. (See the A-Z for warnings!)

The stems can either be annual or biennial. Species with annual stems will die back in the autumn to ground level, where next year's new stem growth buds will already have formed. These will remain visible throughout the winter awaiting suitable conditions from January onwards to burst into life. Species with biennial stems produce evergreen shoots one year, which will over-winter before bearing flowers the following spring. After producing their seed they will die back. It is a natural process for all euphorbias to drop the leaves from the lower half of their stems.

Euphorbias have three different types of leaf. Stem leaves are the most numerous and vary considerably in size and shape, from the diminutive *E. capitulata* with reverse-ovate leaves less than 1 cm long, to the large, almost tropical leaves of *E. stygiana* which has pointed elliptical leaves up to 30cm (1ft) long. Above the stem leaves there is a cluster of leaves known as whorl leaves out of which springs the umbel (the branched flowering head). At the end of the branches, the floral leaves provide the brightest colours. The whorl leaves are usually a different shape and can either be the same colour as the stem leaves or the floral leaves depending on the species. Since the actual flowers of euphorbias are very small and inconspicuous, having neither petals nor sepals, the role of attracting insect pollinators has been taken over by the floral leaves. As the main colour comes from a leaf and not a petal, the colour in most species persists and will maintain garden interest for a considerable length of time.

The make-up of the flower structure is quite complex. Above the floral leaves is a small cup-shaped organ known as a cyathium. Cyathia can occur singly, in pairs, or groups of three. Each cyathium contains an inflorescence that consists of one female flower on a stalk and many male flowers. The male flowers are grouped around the female flower, which develops ahead of the male flowers to avoid self-pollination. On the outside lip of the cup there are nectar glands which can be kidney-shaped or sometimes shaped like a horseshoe. In some species, most notably *E. mellifera*, these glands exude a rich, sweet perfume. The shape and colour of the nectar glands varies from species to species and the colour can range from almost black to brown, buff, yellow, orange and red.

After pollination the seeds are produced in a three-sectioned fruit capsule, each section containing one seed. These capsules are roughly spherical in shape but can vary considerably in appearance from species to species. When a mature capsule dries and shrinks it splits or explodes, sometimes with an audible crack, thus dispersing the seeds in all directions.

Compared with many other herbaceous perennials, euphorbia seeds are fairly large and easy to collect. They range in size from 1.5mm long (*E. portlandica*) to 5mm long (*E. lathyris*) and are usually ovoid in shape. They range in colour from very dark brown through to light brown and into shades of grey. The seeds are hard and mostly smooth. All seeds have a small growth at one end called a caruncle. This is said to contain substances that attract ants, resulting in the ants carrying off the seed, and thus further helping to disperse the seed.

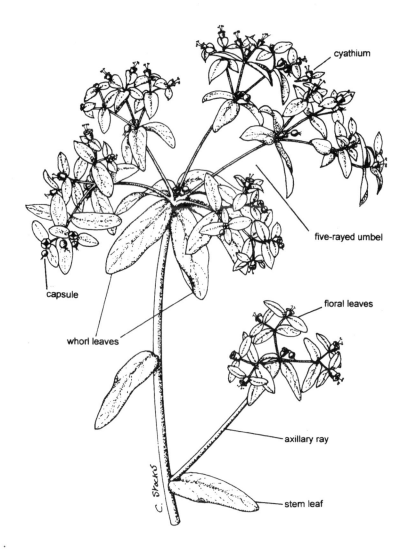

cyathium

five-rayed umbel

floral leaves

capsule

whorl leaves

axillary ray

stem leaf

C. Stocks

The structure of the euphorbia

Euphorbias in the Garden

EUPHORBIAS ARE A VERY VERSATILE group of plants and most garden situations will accommodate a euphorbia or two. The many grey-leaved varieties such as *E. myrsinites* and *E. nicaeensis* like hot, sunny, well-drained positions whilst *E. palustris*, as the name suggests, revels in damp conditions. On heavier clay soils *E. griffithii* and *E. sikkimensis* thrive and remain relatively compact, but on lighter soils they can spread quite quickly. Our native wood spurge *E. amygdaloides* prefers dappled shade and a richer soil and *E. amygdaloides* var. *robbiae* will grow, flourish and flower in deep shade. The miniature *E. capitulata* is a perfect rockery plant whilst *Euphorbia characias* subsp. *wulfenii* var. *sibthorpii* is as big as its name and makes a striking focal point if one has the space.

CULTIVATION

In order to grow good strong specimens of euphorbias it is important to give them growing conditions in the garden which match as closely as possible the conditions where they occur in the wild. This is a truism for most garden plants. As has already been stated, euphorbias are very diverse and can be found in a variety of habitats and climates but, to their credit, most euphorbias are very versatile and will cope with garden conditions that are not ideal for them. For example, many *E. characias* plants may be seen up and down the country growing in the shade of hedges and trees. They manage to grow but, being sun lovers, never reach their potential, as shoot production and flowering is reduced.

In general all euphorbias will be happy with some sun, shelter and reasonable drainage. Even *E. amygdaloides* and its cultivars cope out in the sun and species from around the Mediterranean will be happiest if they can see the sun all day.

Ordinary, loamy garden soil will suit euphorbias providing it doesn't get waterlogged. If the soil is thin or heavy plenty of well-rotted manure or compost should be incorporated before planting. They will tolerate a wide range of pH values. Most of the writer's euphorbias, which grow in mixed beds, get the same treatment as all the other perennials and shrubs - good ground preparation before planting, digging in one year old manure, and an annual mulch of well rotted manure in spring. The beds also get a dressing of general fertiliser at this time and these treatments are certainly rewarded with very good results. The exceptions to this rule are the glaucous leaved varieties that inhabit thin, free-draining soil such as *E. rigida* and *E. capitulata*. These require sharp grit incorporating into the soil prior to planting instead of humus. Some of the rarer plants that the writer has of this type are grown in a slightly raised bed and the soil has been deeply dug (two spits) with plenty of sharp grit added. The whole border is then mulched with grit and it looks good and performs exceptionally well.

Once the roots are happy, the main enemy of the evergreen varieties in winter is the wind. Older plants of *E. characias* and its cultivars can become quite woody at their base and it is not unknown for them to split at the bottom and for whole stems to break off in severe winter gales. This can be countered to a large degree by providing a sheltered environment in the garden by means of plants and buildings. Young plants are especially susceptible to cold winds and in order to get any fragile plants through their first couple of winters outside it can be helpful to erect a fleece barrier around the plant using canes and pegs, leaving the top of the plant open. This has proved most successful on the writer's fairly exposed garden, which is at an altitude of 125m (400+ft) on the eastern edge of the Pennines.

Snow, when it falls can also be a problem. It is not only the cold but the weight of the snow which can cause the damage by bending and breaking evergreen stems and new shoots. The snow should be carefully knocked off as soon as possible, before it goes crisp, and then the stems teased upright. They may look a little sad but will make surprisingly quick recoveries once the snow has gone.

Apart from newly-planted euphorbias, which need watering until they are established - especially if the weather remains dry, it is not necessary to water the plants; they cope very well with dry spells and manage adequately with whatever rainfall is available.

Considering that there are several euphorbias that grow to around a metre or more, a relatively small number of species require staking. The old adage of growing tall plants together so that they help support each other does help but even so, species like *E. palustris*, *E. villosa*, *E. virgata* and *E. esula* cannot support themselves and need staking to prevent them becoming too straggly in the latter half of the season. Whatever method of staking is adopted, the stakes need to be in place early so that the plants can grow above them and look more natural later in the season.

A more detailed list of garden tasks and when to do them can be found on pages 53-55.

12

PESTS AND DISEASES

Compared with many other garden perennials, euphorbias are fairly trouble free. Greenfly can be found on cuttings and young immature plants but once plants are established they are noticeable by their absence, apart from on the growing tips of *E. characias* and its cultivars in spring. The odd whitefly may be found on the underside of a leaf but they are hardly noticeable and like the greenfly appear to have no detrimental effect on growth. The writer has had the odd slug devour the top of a cutting while it is rooting but doesn't know whether these lived to tell the tale; this annoying pest appears never to have attacked euphorbias in the garden.

In the writer's experience, *E. characias* and *E. cyparissias* species and cultivars may suffer from rust, the main effect being that the plants defoliate rather more than they would in a normal year. The worst problem that some euphorbias have is undoubtedly powdery mildew. The vulnerable species are *E. amygdaloides* (especially the cultivar *E. a.* 'Purpurea'), *E.* x *martinii*, *E. dulcis* and *E. sikkimensis* and, to a lesser extent, some cultivars of *E. polychroma, E. cyparissias* and *E. griffithii* New growth is not usually affected and it only becomes a problem later in the season when the main flowering period is over. Gardeners who live east of a line roughly from the Wash to the Isle of Portland may find that mildew is not much of a problem at all.

All these problems can be lessened by spraying if it is deemed necessary. Many gardeners will prefer to let nature look after itself, practise good garden hygiene and not consider that any of these problems significantly diminish the overall effect in a well-grown garden bed.

PLANT ASSOCIATIONS

This is a very individual subject, for what may please one person's eye, may not suit the eye of another. There are, however, one or two rules of thumb and those who do not get it right first time should not be afraid to move plants around until the picture looks good. With the exception of *E characias* and its cultivars euphorbias do not mind being moved (at the right time).

The best colour to associate with euphorbia yellow is undoubtedly blue and deeper shades into purple. The problem is, as already stated, that many herbaceous plants are barely awake, never mind flowering at this time of year. However there are some good varieties of *Iris pallida* and *I. sibirica* that fit the bill and give some height to the border at the appropriate time. Lower growing and making a good ground cover foil are the ajugas with their spikes of rich blue flowers, and aubrieta in a variety of shades of blue. *E. polychroma* and *Brunnera macrophylla* make a pleasing combination in April as does *E. amygdaloides* 'Purpurea' and *Pulmonaria* 'Smokey Blue'. Help can be given here from spring flowering bulbs; blue crocuses look particularly good with one of the first euphorbias to flower, *E. rigida* and *E. rigida* 'Sardis'. Slightly later, blue muscari and hyacinths contrast well with yellow flowering cultivars of *E. characias* and *E. amygdaloides*. As a change, dwarf red tulips look splendid when associated with the lime-green flowers and blue-grey leaves of *E. myrsinites*. Other flowers on the blue spectrum that are around at this time are *Pulsatilla vulgaris* and *Erysimum* 'Bowles' Mauve'. Among the later flowering euphorbia species there is more choice of blue. Here are some examples: *E. donii* and blue leaved hostas - especially *H.* 'Halcyon'; *E. nicaeensis* and *Campanula carpatica; E. cornigera* and blue flowering monardas (try *M.* 'Blaustrumpf' (syn. Blue Stocking) or *M.* 'Prärienacht' (Prairie Night); *E. seguieriana* subsp. *niciciana* and *Geranium renardii.*

The second general rule is to avoid pink flowers with the fiery colours of *E. griffithii* and its cultivars. They do not make a pleasing combination.

Growing a lot of euphorbias together may not be found to give a pleasing result - it would be too much in spring and the whole area would lack substance in summer. They really need to be part of an overall planting scheme with different genera enhancing and complementing each other. However, the red of *E. griffithii* goes very well alongside euphorbia yellow if one wants a clump of hot, vibrant colour early in the season. The writer grows *E. grffithii* 'Dixter', *E. ceratocarpa* and *Geranium* 'Ann Folkard' together in a fairly close triangle. The two spring flowering euphorbias are guaranteed to attract visitors' attention with the vermilion red of *E.g.* 'Dixter' intermingled with the acid yellow flowers of *E. ceratocarpa*. After they have flowered there is plenty of strong leaf colour and height for *G.* 'Ann Folkard' to scramble through and flower throughout the summer. Another way of growing a number of euphorbias together is in a scree bed. Short species that are ideally suited for this are *E. acanthothamnos, E. capitulata, E. myrsinites, E. rigida* and *E. spinosa*. If these are inter-planted with a variety of dwarf sedums, e.g. *S. cauticola* and *S. spathulifolium;* sempervivums, e.g. *Sempervivum arachnoideum;* and *Iris reticulata,* the overall effect will make a very pleasing feature for a sunny spot in any garden.

CUT FLOWERS

It is a little known fact that euphorbias make very good cut flowers as they will last a considerable length of time in water. A vase of *E. characias* stems makes a floriferous and unusual display, or they can be mixed with other types of cut flowers to add stature. Other suitable euphorbias with strong stems include *E. schillingii, E. donii, E. griffithii, E.* x *martinii* and *E. nicaeensis.* Perhaps the reason why they are not so well used is the problem encountered with the sap. This can be lessened by gently pushing the end of the stems into the soil immediately after cutting, thereby staunching the flow of the sap.

Flower arrangers certainly find euphorbias desirable in their designs as the writer is often asked for plants specifically for this purpose. Perhaps the most popular species used in flower arranging is *E. marginata.*

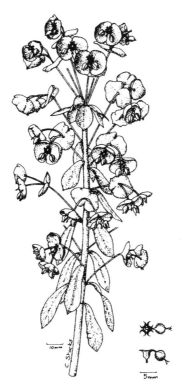

Euphorbia x martinii

15

Propagation

WHEN IT COMES TO PROPAGATION garden euphorbias can be something of an enigma. With some species propagation is easy, the main problem being how to restrain them, whilst other varieties (notably *E. characias* cultivars) can prove decidedly difficult. Three methods of propagation can be employed: seed, cuttings and division. Some cultivars will produce good viable garden plants from seed but they may be variable and not come true to type. Most named cultivars must be propagated by vegetative means i.e. cuttings and division, though *E. amygdaloides* 'Purpurea', *E dulcis* 'Chameleon', *E. marginata* 'Summer Icicle' and *E. rigida* 'Sardis' are raised from seed. With these, any less strongly coloured or less variegated seedlings should be rogued out.

SEED

Seed can be sown any time from the end of February onwards, in pots under glass or in a seedbed in a cold frame. If heat is used, germination is quick and seedlings will soon need pricking out. With use of heat it is very difficult to get even growth and, if the resulting seedlings are not attended to at the right moment, plants can quite quickly become leggy. Seeds sown from April onwards don't even need covering, provided they are watered regularly. Whatever time seeds are sown, they should be covered with about 1cm of sharp grit or horticultural sand. This tends not to form as hard a crust as does soil or compost and germinating seeds have less of a problem pushing through. Germination time is fairly quick and most seeds should be through well within four weeks. As soon as the seedlings are large enough to handle, with true leaves developed, prick them out into pots. Grow on and plant out into their final positions when a good root system has developed. Rarer and more tender species are better potted on into larger pots in the summer, over-wintered in an unheated greenhouse or cold frame for the first winter and planted out the following spring. Cover with fleece during the winter if really cold weather is forecast. This will ensure a stronger larger plant that will be more able to fend for itself during its first winter outside.

Collecting seed is quite straightforward. Many species produce a succession of seed over a period of time. Species such as *E. characias* are ready from June onwards. Others produce ripe seed at varying times through the summer and some as late as October. Cut the stems containing mature seed capsules, with flowers absent, when the large plump fruits are turning a dull green to brown (they start to crack on warm sunny days when ripe). Place them in a large paper bag, label it, and leave it in a dry place until the end of the season. By this time viable seed will have split from the dried fruit shell and will be at the bottom of the bag. Separate the seed from the debris. This is a good, (if tedious) job to do with the onset of the dark evenings in late September and October. Store the seed in paper envelopes in the refrigerator during the winter.

CUTTINGS

The best time to take stem cuttings is from April to July. Use a sharp knife and cut 8-10cm (3-4in) shoots from healthy new growth and remove the lower leaves. This process can produce copious amounts of sap. Staunch the flow by gently pressing the cut end into soil. Alternatively drop the cutting into a container of water (this method is useful when collecting a large number of cuttings of one cultivar). Wearing surgical rubber gloves prevents the sap from making any contact with the skin. Standard procedure is to use hormone rooting powder and strike the cuttings in a mix of 50-50 peat/horticultural sharp sand but some gardeners may have their own recipes and preferences.

It is very important to control the humidity around the leaves. Many euphorbia species and cultivars, unlike cuttings of most other plants, cope very well without being covered. Provided they are kept out of the sun and are well watered, they hardly wilt and disease and rotting is much reduced. However, large leafy clump-forming spurges, such as *E. palustris, E. villosa, E. oblongata, E. soongarica, E. griffithii* and its cultivars, all benefit from being covered for a week or two. Keep a close eye on them and remove the cover when cuttings are established. Most other cuttings will do better without a cover. The secret lies in keeping their feet moist and their heads (the leaves) dry. This is especially so when dealing with cuttings of *E. characias* cultivars, as poor results are obtained if the leaves remain damp for any length of time. *E. characias* cuttings can also be slow to produce a good root system so it is best to take these as early as possible when the material is available - April and May.

New growth being produced at the top of the stem is an indication that the cuttings have struck. Pot them up from the end of July onwards and pot them on again if necessary in September. Over-

17

winter them under glass. Grow on the following spring and plant out when they have reached a good size.

There is an alternative way to propagate *E. characias* cultivars, which have a variable success rate when propagated from tip cuttings. Take 30cm (1ft) stems with a sharp knife in summer. Strip the leaves from the lower half of each and treat it like a hardwood cutting. Insert the lower half into the soil outside with a little sand in the bottom of the hole. Water regularly and these cuttings will cope well with the hot summer sun. Leave in the ground over winter. Dig up and pot up the following spring. Expect some losses but on the whole results are satisfactory.

DIVISION

Division is the easiest method of propagation with running varieties such as *E. cyparissias, E. virgata, E. esula* and *E. amygdaloides* var. *robbiae.* Just dig pieces up in late winter and early spring and plant them up either in a pot or in their new position. The roots are not deep and plants are easy to dig up and divide. New shoots of *E. griffithii* and *E. sikkimensis,* which can appear some way from the main clump, can be sliced off using a spade and potted up. Despite having very few fine roots, they will root quickly if kept watered.

Tighter clump-forming euphorbias such as *E. polychroma, E. oblongata* and *E. villosa* can be split in half with a spade if the clump gets too big. February is the best time to do this, before too much top growth develops. If necessary, these clumps can be split into several smaller pieces and potted up. The crowns can get quite woody so a sharp knife will be handy. Providing there is at least one growth bud and a piece of root joined, and they are kept well watered, they will soon grow away happily. Odd pieces of *E. polychroma* with no apparent roots have been known to manage to develop into strong plants after being put into pots. A fair sized clump that has been divided and transplanted straight back into the garden will have lost quite a bit of its root system. Such divisions should be kept well watered until they are established, especially if the weather is dry in spring. Large leafy species like *E. palustris* are unlikely to grow to their full size the first year after transplanting.

E. characias and cultivars, although looking and growing like a clump forming perennial have in fact a central taproot and will not propagate by division.

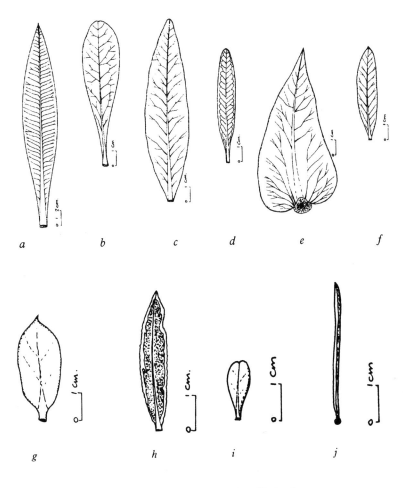

a	E. sikkimensis
b.	E. lathyris
c.	E. jacquemontii
d.	E. stygiana
e.	E. amygdaloides var. robbiae

f.	E. donii
g.	E. myrsinites
h.	E. polychroma 'Lacy'
i.	E. capitulata
j.	E. cyparissias

Euphorbia leaf shapes and sizes

Euphorbias: an alphabetical listing

HERE IS AN ALPHABETICAL LIST of euphorbia species and cultivars that the gardener should be able to acquire. Many are easy to obtain; others will take some finding and may only be available at odd times. All can be cultivated outside in Britain - depending on local climate, soil and available shelter. The species are usually reliably named in the trade with the exception of *E. wallichii* (see entry) but cultivar varieties - especially those of *E. characias, E. cyparissias* and *E. griffithii* are very confused. Some named cultivars may differ slightly from the descriptions given, depending on the source of the plant. Some species appear under synonyms, particularly the following:

E. biglandulosa - see *E. rigida*
E. epithymoides - see *E. polychroma*
E. longifolia - see *E. donii*
E. reflexa - see *E. seguieriana* subsp. *niciciana*
E. serrulata - see *E. stricta*
E. uralensis - see *E. x pseudovirgata*
E. x waldsteinii - see *E. virgata.*
E. stricta has the commercial name *E.* Golden Foam.

E. acanthothamnos (spiny spurge) Z9   Greece/Turkey
An odd looking plant, this grows into a rounded prickly hummock up to 60cm (2ft). It has small shrubby stems with very small leaves that, unusually, disappear in the summer, new ones re-growing for the winter. The plant is covered with a mass of tiny yellow flowers in March and April. It needs a well-drained and protected site. A not very hardy shrub suitable for a rock garden or scree bed. Propagate from seed.

E. altissima Z9   Middle East
A clump-forming perennial with long, narrow, pointed mid-green leaves. The stems are annual with a downy texture. Lime-yellow flowers are present from May to July. It is only moderately hardy and needs a well-drained rich soil in a border with a protected position. Propagate from seed or by division. 90cm (3ft).

E. amygdaloides (wood spurge) Z6   Europe
A British native that reaches around 75cm (45in) but can be smaller

depending on soil and situation. Preferring dappled shade, it inhabits open woodland but will tolerate sun. It prefers a rich but well-drained soil. The wild British form has darkish-green, hairy, evergreen leaves with a hint of purple. Stems are pinkish; lime-green flowers appear from March to June. Propagation is easy from seed but cultivars need to be propagated vegetatively. Some cultivars can suffer from mildew after flowering. They are all fairly short-lived clump-forming perennials.

E. amygdaloides 'Craigieburn' — Garden Origin
Introduced from Craigieburn garden in Scotland and perhaps the best form of *E. amygdaloides*. Many upright stems, clothed in port-coloured leaves, are topped with clear light yellow flowers in April and May. A first rate plant for the front of the border. 50cm (20in).

E. amygdaloides 'Purpurea' (syn. *E.a.* 'Rubra') AGM Garden Origin
There is a wide variation in the quality and colour of plants offered under this name. The best forms are well worth growing. Maroon stems carry beetroot-red evergreen leaves that look very attractive, especially during the winter. Yellow flowers appear from March to May. Prefers a good garden soil with some sun. Suffers from mildew later in the season and can become a little straggly. 60cm (2ft).

E. amygdaloides var. *robbiae* (Mrs Robb's bonnet) AGM Z6
Introduced from Turkey by Mary Robb in 1891. Flowering time, structure and colour are as the wild British form but the leaves and habit are sufficiently different for some authors to consider it a separate species. It varies in height from 60-90cm (2-3ft), spreading outwards by underground runners - often leaving bare patches in the middle. Dark green rounded, shiny, evergreen leaves have a leathery texture. Lime-green flowers are produced from March to May. Propagation is easy by division and, as stems become woody with age, it is best dug up and fresh growth replanted in tight clumps every 2-3 years. A very robust plant that will tolerate most soils and aspects, including deep shade; it will provide ground cover in dark inhospitable places for a great deal longer than three years.

E. amygdaloides var. *robbiae* 'Pom Pom' — Garden Origin
A recent introduction from Bob Brown. A smaller, more compact version of its parent with small leaves in tight pom-pom like shoots. It is less invasive than *E.a.* var. *robbiae* and makes an attractive evergreen clump. 30cm (12in).

E. amygdaloides 'Variegata' Z8-9   Garden Origin
An attractive variegated leaved form. Less hardy than the species.
Unfortunately it has a weak constitution and soon dies.

E. baselicis (E. barrelieri) Z9   Mediterranean
Smooth, greyish-blue evergreen leaves. Lime-yellow flowers appear in
June and July. A small plant with a floppy, open, untidy habit. It
needs a well-drained soil in a warm sheltered site and even then may
not survive a harsh winter. A clump-forming perennial suitable for a
scree bed or the front of the border. Raise new plants from seed.
40cm (16in).

E. boissieriana Z6   Asia
Mid-green deciduous leaves. Yellow-green flowers appear in June and
July. Similar to *E. virgata* but more robust. Any soil in sun or part
shade. A running perennial. 1m (39in).

E. brittingeri (syn. E. flavicoma) Z8   Mediterranean Europe
A small, variable species. Green leaves on annual pinkish stems turn
orange in autumn. Lime-yellow flowers appear from June to
September. Needs a gritty free draining soil in full sun. A clump-
forming perennial for the front of the border. 30cm (1ft).

E. broteroi (Brotero's spurge) Z10   Iberian Peninsular
Robust upward-arching stems have light bluish evergreen leaves. In
March and April yellow-green floral leaves are produced with orange-
scarlet nectaries. Give it a sheltered position in free-draining stony
soil. The leaves dislike contact with soil so it is best to mulch around
the plant with gravel. Propagate from seed. 35cm (14in).

E. capitulata Z8   Balkans
A very unusual spurge as it is tiny, reaching only 10cm (4in) in height.
It needs a free-draining soil and a sunny aspect and is suitable for
troughs and rock gardens. Prostrate stems carry small grey-green
evergreen leaves. Minute flowers yellow, turning orange, appear from
March to May. A slowly spreading clump-forming perennial. Best
propagated in spring by carefully cutting off a small portion from the
main clump and potting up.

E. ceratocarpa Z8   Italy/Sicily
An interesting species with wiry pink stems that become woody with
age. It has narrow blue-green leaves on annual stems and heads of
frothy euphorbia-yellow flowers. This is one of the longest flowering
perennials in the garden. With careful pruning it will flower for ten

months starting in March with peak flowering from April to June. Any soil in a sunny sheltered position. A perennial sub shrub suitable for the middle of the border. 90cm (3ft).

E. characias Z7   Mediterranean

This spurge makes a very distinctive garden plant whether it is in leaf or flower. An evergreen, clump-forming perennial of some stature, it is justifiably one of the best and most popular euphorbia species. The leaves come in shades of blue or green and clothe thick, strong, pale green stems. Coming from the Mediterranean region, all plants enjoy plenty of sunshine. They will grow in ordinary or thin garden soil and being tap rooted will tolerate quite dry conditions. This tap root does mean however that, apart from the subspecies which do come true from seed, the only method of propagation for cultivars is from cuttings, which is often not easy (see section on propagation). *E. characias* does seed around readily and this has resulted in many crosses. There are now many named cultivars with different leaves, nectaries and heights. Some of these cultivars are very distinct and make excellent garden plants. However some named cultivars show no significant differences from several others and this has caused some confusion.

All species and cultivars of *E. characias* should have their flowering stems cut back as near to the base as possible in June and July after the flowers have died. This is not an easy job, especially with the larger cultivars and over the years a mound of dead woody stumps will develop and the number of flowering stems will diminish. For this reason *E. characias* plants have a useful life span of around ten years depending on growing conditions and on the care and maintenance given by the gardener.

E. characias should be hardy, but does not like cold winter gales or heavy wet soils, which may kill off plants - especially older weaker specimens. In winter the leaves will droop and become limp in frosty conditions. Just before flowering in late winter, the flowering stem tips bend over and face downwards. Then, just before the flower buds open, they turn upright again and produce wonderfully varied and coloured flower heads. If flowering stems are left, most cultivars will produce small shoots in the flowerhead by late summer that are extremely easy to root (even as late as the end of September); this can be a useful means of increasing choice clones quickly.

It is a variable species in the wild and there are two distinct subspecies. However, these have also hybridised in cultivation, sometimes making it difficult to determine in which subspecies a cultivar belongs. Smaller cultivars make excellent front of the border plants whilst the majority look good in the middle of mixed borders. The larger plants will make fine focal points in any garden.

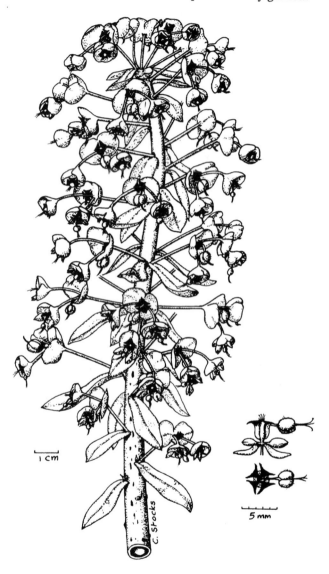

Euphorbia characias

E. characias subsp. ***characias*** AGM   Western Mediterranean
This is the shorter of the two subspecies, usually only up to 1m
(39in). The leaves are light olive green. The nectaries are dark brown
or dark purple inside the flowers, which are produced from February
to May. It may repeat flower from September - November.

E. characias subsp. ***wulfenii*** AGM   Eastern Mediterranean
The taller of the two subspecies reaching as high as 1.8m (6ft) but
often less. It has longer leaves that are a pale glaucous blue. The
nectaries are much lighter in colour, being light brown, buff or yellow.
Generally, cultivars that have evolved from subsp. characias are
shorter more compact plants than cultivars with the wulfenii genes in
their blood.

E. characias 'Amber Eye'   Garden Origin
A diminutive form of *characias* from Gary Dunlop's garden. It is
barely 60cm (2ft) tall and produces only a small number of stems with
mid-green leaves. However, these stems are crammed full of bright gold,
frog-spawn-like floral heads with amber centres, in March and April.

E. characias 'Black Pearl'   Garden Origin
A new compact variety with dull green leaves. The floral leaves in
March and April are lime green with very dark brown, almost black,
nectaries. 75cm (30in).

E. characias subsp. ***characias*** 'Blue Hills'   Garden Origin
An excellent cultivar having dense, blue-grey, pointed evergreen
foliage that looks good throughout the winter months. Lime green
floral heads with brown centres appear from March to May. 60cm (2ft).

E. characias subsp. ***characias*** 'Burrow Silver'   Garden Origin
Raised by Mary Benger of Burrow Farm Garden near Axminster.
This is a handsome variegated-leaf form having creamy white edges to
the leaves and light green centres. It is quite a tall upright variety at
90cm (3ft). The floral leaves can be almost all cream. Unfortunately
this plant has a weak constitution and cold and wet conditions cause
die-back and the leaves turn brown.

E. characias dwarf   Garden Origin
Closely packed, rounded, blue-grey evergreen leaves that have an
unusual hairy texture. Tightly packed green floral leaves with dark
brown centres appear from April to May. An attractive compact plant
which benefits from some shelter from the winter rain as the leaves
hold the wet and this can cause rotting of the shoot tips. An ideal

front of the border plant. 60cm (2ft).

E. characias 'Goldbrook'   Garden Origin
Long pale-grey evergreen foliage. Large heads of pale yellow floral leaves with buff centres, darkening to purple with age, appear from March to May. Very similar to some forms of *E. wulfenii* but smaller. 90cm (3ft).

E. characias subsp. characias 'Green Mantle'   Garden Origin
An unusual and eye-catching introduction from Gary Dunlop. Stem leaves are a strikingly rich green colour and pointed. The floral leaves are strangely the same colour green as the stem leaves with dark maroon brown nectaries. 1m (39in).

E. characias subsp. characias 'H.E. Bates'   Garden Origin
The young growth is purple turning green. Yellow flowers with reddish-brown nectaries in spring. Selected by Mr Bates and introduced by Christopher Lloyd.

E. characias subsp. characias 'Humpty Dumpty' Garden Origin
A very popular variety introduced by Pat Perry of Whitby. It has a neat dumpy habit producing a vast number of stems (it is not unusual to see 80 or more flowering stems). Bright, grey-green leaves are topped with apple green flowers with light brown centres that appear from February to May. An excellent border plant. 1.1m (3½ft).

E. characias subsp. characias 'Kestrel'   Garden Origin
Linear leaves with margins and midrib of the palest cream (paler than 'Burrow Silver'). The floral heads are striking, with floral leaves of the same very pale cream. A relatively vigorous plant reaching around 75cm (30in) in height. It appeared as a chance seedling at Kestrel Cottage, Brand Green, Gloucestershire.

E. characias subsp. characias 'Percy Picton'   Garden Origin
Tall upright stems carry plain, blue-green leaves. Flowers produced in March and April are unusual in that the floral leaves are variegated. 1m (39in).

E. characias subsp. characias 'Perry's Winter Blusher' Garden Origin
An interesting introduction from Pat Perry of Whitby. Long, green, over-wintering leaves. Long flowering stems carry green floral heads that hang down exposing a distinctive orange-red flush on the outside. The main flowering time is February to May, but it is known to produce some floral display from October onwards. The flowering stems are quite lax and flop outwards slightly giving it an open habit. 1m (39in).

E. characacias 'Portuguese Velvet'

Portugal

A relatively new cultivar, collected in Portugal by John Fielding, which has deep green, rounded evergreen leaves with a very soft, smooth, velvety texture. Heads of green flowers with brown centres appear from March - May. 90cm (3ft).

E. characacias 'Sombre Melody'

Garden Origin

A relatively new introduction by Gary Dunlop and a very unusual and highly decorative plant. The fairly small floral heads are tightly packed with flowers of an unusual colouring. The floral leaves are pale green with a slight browny/pink tinge. Nectaries are dark brown through to orange and yellow and the various colours occur simultaneously. Strong, tall, upright stems carry numerous tightly packed mid-green leaves. Clear yellow floral heads appear from March to May. 1.1m (3½ft).

E. characacias 'Spring Splendour'

Garden Origin

A relatively new introduction. Strong, tall, upright stems carry numerous tightly packed mid-green leaves. Clear yellow floral heads appear from March to May. 1.1m (3½ft).

E. characacias 'Variegata'

This is the name given to any variegated seedlings thrown up from 'Lambrook Gold'. They generally make good garden plants but can vary in flower, height and leaf variegation. 60-100cm (24-40in).

E. characacias 'Whistleberry Gold'

Garden Origin

Light green-blue leaves on spreading stems. Cylindrical flower heads carry yellow flowers in March and April. 75cm (30in).

E. characacias 'Whistleberry Jade'

Garden Origin

Light blue-green leaves on upright stems reaching 1m (39in). Jade-green flower heads are produced in March and April.

E. characacias subsp. *wulfenii* 'Bosahan'

Garden Origin

Very thick strong stems carry long pale glaucous blue leaves. Large, broad, pale yellow flower heads are produced in March and April. The floral leaves have a pink hue after flowering and maintain colour and interest well into summer. Found in a Cornish garden of the same name. 1m (39in).

E. characacias subsp. *wulfenii* 'Emmer Green'

Garden Origin

Perhaps the strongest and best of the variegated characacias cultivars, this occurred as a sporting shoot in a garden in the village of Emmer Green in Berkshire. It has green pointed leaves with a thick cream margin on pink tinged stems. The floral heads in March and April are also variegated. It still needs protection but copes better with the cold and wet. An excellent but rare variety. 1m (39in).

E. charicias subsp. **wulfenii 'Jimmy Platt'**   Garden Origin
A relatively new variety introduced by Jimmy Platt who was assistant editor on the RHS *Journal*. It is a shrubby evergreen with mid-green leaves. A particularly floriferous variety producing tall stems of tightly packed dull yellow floral heads that have red cyathia. 90cm (3ft).

E. charicias subsp. **wulfenii 'John Tomlinson'** AGM Yugoslavia
Tends not to produce as many flowering stems as some other varieties. Still worth growing for its blue-grey leaves and its distinct large ball-shaped clusters of glowing yellow flowers that appear from February to May. Any soil in sun. Collected in the wild, seedlings are often equally as good as the parent. 1m (39in).

E. charicias subsp. **wulfenii 'Lambrook Gold'** AGM Garden Origin
An excellent and very popular variety introduced by Margery Fish. Greyish to pale green evergreen foliage with a tendency to produce odd stems with some variegation in the leaves. Large heads of golden yellow flowers top the plant from March to May. Any well-drained soil in sun. Propagate from cuttings. Seedlings belong to the Margery Fish Group; some may produce variegated forms. 1m (39in).

E. charicias subsp. **wulfenii 'Lambrook Yellow'**   Garden Origin
A descendant of 'Lambrook Gold'. Bluish evergreen foliage. Large floral heads bearing lime-yellow flowers with pale brown centres appear in March and April. It may repeat flower in October and November. Any well-drained soil in sun. 1m (39in).

E. charicias subsp. **wulfenii Margery Fish Group**
A name given to seedlings raised from *E*. 'Lambrook Gold'. Plants seen under this name can be quite variable.

E. charicias subsp. **wulfenii 'Perry's Tangerine'**   Garden Origin
Another of Pat Perry's introductions, this cultivar is a strong upright plant that produces a lot of stems that carry densely packed blue-green leaves. Tangerine coloured flowers appear from March to May. Any soil in sun. 1.1m (3½ft).

E. charicias subsp. **wulfenii 'Purple and Gold'**
(syn. E.c. subsp. wulfenii 'Purpurea')   Garden Origin
A stunning plant with a long period of interest. It has plain green leaves during the summer, but from the first frosts in October the upper leaves on every stem turn a rich purple, and remain so, giving

28

colour and interest throughout the dark winter days. The finale occurs from February to May when large, rich, bright yellow flowers top the stems and contrast superbly against the dark purple foliage. After that the leaves fade back to green anonymity for another summer. Any soil in sun. 1.2m (4ft).

E. characias subsp. *wulfenii* var. *sibthorpii*   Greece
This is the name given to the Greek wild variety of *E. wulfenii*. It is a large plant with mid-green over-wintering leaves. Large yellow flower heads are produced from February to May. It needs a lot of space to reach its potential size. Any soil in sun. A large clump-forming perennial sub shrub. Height and spread up to 1.6m (4½ft).

E. characias subsp. *wulfenii* 'Thelma's Giant'   Garden Origin
Long blue-green leaves on tall stems with a slight pink tinge. Large open well-spaced out flowers are produced in March and April with light yellow floral leaves and nectaries. 1.2m (4ft).

E. cognata Z7   Pakistan/Afghanistan
Mid-green deciduous leaves with a downy texture and a faint maroon edge are carried on pink stems. Yellow flowers from July to September. Normal garden soil in sun or part shade. A clump-forming perennial similar to *E. cornigera*. Propagate from seed. 75cm (30in).

E. corallioides (coral spurge) Z7   Italy/Sicily
Daintily branched, coral pink stems with mid-green hairy evergreen leaves with a coral-red or brownish tint. It has an open habit topped with green floral heads with tiny yellow flowers from May to July. It will self-seed a little and therefore propagation is easy from seed. Ordinary soil in sun or part shade. A short-lived perennial or biennial. 1m (39in).

E. cornigera Z7   Pakistan/N. India
Pale green leaves on annual stems with branched yellow flower heads from June to August. A plant with an open habit that may need staking. Prefers a richer soil in sun or part shade. A popular clump-forming perennial, up to 1m (39in). Any plant labelled *E. wallichii* that grows taller than 60cm (2ft) is more likely to be *E. cornigera*. (See *E. wallichii*.)

E.. cyparissias (cypress spurge) Z5   Europe - Central Asia
This species produces a mass of small, mid-green, narrow foliage on thin annual stems. Lime-yellow floral heads around 40cm (16in) high are produced from April to June. The flowers have a sweet aroma although this is usually only detectable at ground level. Any garden

soil in sun or part shade. A dainty plant but unfortunately it spreads in all directions, more so on lighter soils. Easy to propagate by division but not so easy to control, especially if it runs among other plants or into paving. Named cultivars all have a similar habit and need to be placed carefully - in a wild garden, in amongst tough shrubs, or in a pot.

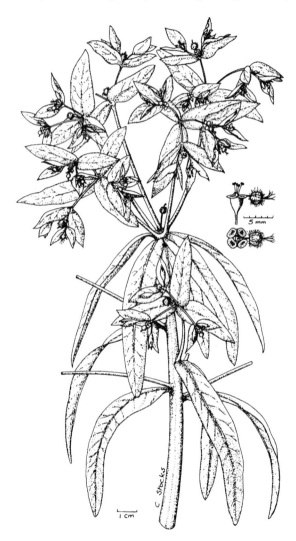

Euphorbia coralloides

E. cyparissias 'Ashfield'   Garden Origin
Found in Mary Hargreaves' garden near Bradford. Flower colour and
time are the same as the species but the plant is smaller in height at
20-25cm (8-10in). The slowest-spreading cultivar.

E. cyparissias 'Baby'   Wild montane form
A miniature version of the species growing only to 15cm (6in). The
stem leaves are very densely packed along the stem, which does not
branch.

E. cyparissias 'Bushman Boy'   Garden Origin
First called 'Bush Boy' by Gary Dunlop who introduced it, it is a
much branched form giving a very feathery appearance. Otherwise
similar in habit and flower to the species, but smaller. 20cm (8in).

E. cyparissias 'Clarice Howard' (syn. E.c. 'Purpurea') Garden Origin
New stems in spring are covered in handsome deep purple or maroon
leaves. The tiny clusters of frothy yellow flowers from April to June
look particularly attractive against the leaves. It can have a second
flush of leaves and some flowers in September and October. 45cm
(18in). Found in a West Yorkshire garden by Howard Bateman.

E. cyparissias 'Fens Ruby'   Garden Origin
New leaves in spring are lighter purple than E.c. 'Clarice Howard'
becoming paler and greener with age. It has the usual flower colour
but is slightly taller than most other forms at 45cm (18in). It will
produce a second flush of flower and leaves in September and
October.

E. cyparissias 'Orange Man'   Garden Origin
Floral leaves have a yellow-orange tint from April to June. The
branched stems are over in autumn and leaves die off in shades of
orange. One of the best varieties of E. cyparissias but a real thug in the
garden, so a neat tidy gardener wanting to grow this should imprison
it in a container. 40cm (16in).

E. cyparissias 'Red Devil'   Garden Origin
Small, dainty foliage on annual stems. Young leaves are deep purple,
fading to green with age. Lime-yellow flowers from April to June.
May repeat flower in September. Very similar to E.c. 'Fens Ruby' but
smaller at 35cm (14in).

E. cyparissias 'Tall Boy'   Garden Origin
Tall upright annual stems carry long dainty foliage. Interesting floral
heads bearing well-spaced yellow flowers from April to June. The

tallest cultivar at 50cm (20in). Introduced by Gary Dunlop.

E. donii Z7 Himalaya

Very handsome, deep, rich green foliage with dark red edges and a white mid-rib. Dark red annual stems are topped with strong lime-yellow flowers from May to September. It may need staking. Ordinary soil in sun or part shade. A very attractive clump-forming perennial suitable for the middle of the border. Height up to lm (39in). Propagate from seed or cuttings.

E. dulcis Z4 Europe

Plain green rounded leaves on annual stems. Small green floral leaves with a tiny red centre cover the plant from April to May. *E. dulcis* does suffer from mildew but the problem usually only appears after flowering. It has a thick rhizome that is often visible at ground level just above the soil. Any moisture retentive soil in sun or part shade. In a dry soil it may defoliate in early summer. A clump-forming perennial but may seed around. Up to 70cm (28in) but often smaller.

E. dulcis 'Chameleon' France

Rich, purply-brown annual leaves in spring which become purply-green as they age. Tiny yellow flowers flushed with purple cover the plant, giving it a smoky appearance, from March to May. Best in moist soil and full sun. Can be cut down to ground level after flowering and will then produce a new flush of fresh mildew free leaves in late summer. A clump-forming perennial but seeds itself around. 75cm (30in).

E. esula Z7 Europe (South & East)

Lime-yellow flowers appear in May and June. It produces a large number of annual stems bearing mid-green leaves. The stems continue to grow after flowering, reaching around 80cm (32in) and can become very straggly and tangled; this makes staking necessary. Any soil in sun or part shade. A vigorous, running, variable perennial which is easily propagated by division.

E. Excalibur = E. 'Froeup' Z7 Garden Origin

A relatively new introduction, by Fromefield Nursery near Romsey in Hampshire, reputed to be a hybrid between *E. cornigera* and *E. schillingii* and having characteristics of both. It has light red new growth. Grey-green leaves, edged maroon, are produced on pink, annual stems. Yellow flowers from May to August. It may need some support in an exposed position. Best in well-drained soil in sun. A handsome clump-forming perennial for the middle of the border. 90cm (3ft). Propagate by cuttings.

E. glauca (Maori spurge) Z10   New Zealand

Erect stems up to 60cm (2ft) are covered in waxy greyish-blue evergreen leaves. The floral leaves are a glaucous green with dark red/maroon nectaries appearing from May to July. Unfortunately, needing free draining soil and a sunny sheltered spot, it is doubtfully hardy, as it dislikes cold and wet and is only suitable for the mildest locations. In colder areas it can be easily dug up in the autumn, with divisions being potted up and over-wintered in a cool greenhouse before being replanted in the garden the following spring.

E. griffithii (Griffith's spurge) Z5   Himalaya

All forms of this species make first class garden plants. They are an extremely attractive addition to the spring border. The deep red stems are clothed with handsome mid-green leaves on annual stems. Light red flowers develop from March to June. All forms spread by sending up new shoots away from the main crown. However, it is quite easy to control by cutting back. This problem is worse on lighter soils and large clumps can develop if not checked. After flowering, branched stems will continue to grow and overtake the fading flower heads, increasing the plant's height by half as much again. These stems make excellent cutting material in early summer. Alternatively, propagate by division in late winter. Cut back dying stems to ground level in October. Any soil in sun or part shade. 80cm (32in).

E. griffithii 'Dixter' AGM   Garden Origin

Raised by Hilda Davenport-Jones of Washfield Nursery. The leaves of this excellent cultivar are much darker than usual, being deep bloodshot green and pinkish-grey underneath. Dark red stems carry vermilion red floral leaves with yellow nectaries in April and May. Shorter than *E.g.* 'Fireglow' at 60+cm (2ft). A selected seedling introduced by Christopher Lloyd of Great Dixter in Sussex.

E. griffithii 'Dixter Flame'   Garden Origin

A selected form from Gary Dunlop. All the same colours of stem, leaf and flowers as 'Dixter' but a smaller and more compact plant. 60cm (2ft).

E. griffithii 'Fern Cottage'   Garden Origin

A variety discovered by Clive Jones in Cumbria and named after his house. It has burnt orange flowers and good autumn colouring to the leaves. 75cm (30in).

E. griffithii 'Fireglow'   Garden Origin

The commonest of the *E. griffithii* cultivars with pink stems carrying mid-green leaves with pale pink mid ribs. It was originally selected

and introduced by Alan Bloom of Bressingham. The true strain of
E.g. 'Fireglow' has deep, fiery red flowers with yellow centres in April
and May, and are first class border perennials. However plants offered
under this name are variable as many of the plants have been raised
from seed and sometimes one finds some of the rich fieriness has
disappeared from the floral leaves. 85cm (34in).

Euphorbia griffithii **'King's Caple'**

E. griffithii 'King's Caple'   Garden Origin
Introduced by Mrs Taylor of King's Caple, Herefordshire and the
tallest cultivar, reaching 1.1m (40in). As a result it may need staking,
especially if it is in an exposed setting. This should not deter
gardeners from growing this excellent plant, which bears large floral
heads in subtle shades of orange and looks particularly stunning when
illuminated from behind by sunlight.

E. griffithii 'Robert Poland'   Garden Origin
Another excellent variety; a selected form of *E.g.* 'Fireglow' from
Robert Poland, who lived in Sussex. It has good floral colour and
larger, more robust leaves of olive green colour with a reddish
underside. 80cm (32in).

E. griffithii 'Wickstead'   Garden Origin
A variety in between *E.g.* 'Dixter' and *E.g.* 'Fireglow'. It has darker
leaves than the latter but lighter than the former. At around 90cm
(36in) it is also intermediate in height.

E. helioscopia (sun spurge) Z6   Europe - Asia
A hardy annual reaching 30cm (1ft) in height. It propagates itself
easily from seed and has managed to reach every continent as an
introduction. A single erect stem bearing quite attractive lime-green
flowers before turning to seed. It needs managing to prevent it from
becoming a weed.

E. hyberna (Irish spurge) Z6   Western Europe
Mid-green, semi-evergreen leaves on stems that become woody. The
lower stem soon becomes bare and it has a distinct flowering habit of
being very flat topped. Small yellow flowers appear from February to
June. It may then produce a second flush of flowers in the autumn.
Any soil in sun or part shade. It produces an abundance of seed and
will seed around if not dead-headed. A fairly short-lived clump-
forming perennial, ideal for an informal garden. 75cm (30in).

E. jacquemontii (Jacquemont's spurge) Z7   Himalaya
An unusual leafy, clump-forming perennial for the front half of the
border. Long blue-green leaves with maroon edges and white midribs
are borne on annual stems. Pale yellow flowers appear on branched
stems from May to July. It requires a good soil in a sunny sheltered
spot. Propagate from seed or cuttings. 60cm (2ft).

E. lathyris (Mediterranean caper spurge) Z7   Mediterranean
A most unusual euphorbia with a strangely curious appearance. Its
unique habit, with stiff upward-pointing leaves of glossy olive green

1 cm.

5mm

C. Stocks

Euphorbia hyberna

with a fleshy texture, give it a look like no other garden spurge. Young growth is a single stem which becomes progressively more branched as the plant ages. Large, unusually shaped, green floral leaves with small yellow centres appear from May onwards. It produces masses of large fruit and seed. Self-sown seedlings will appear around the garden. It prefers a well-drained soil and sunny aspect to reach its full size but some gardeners will be happy to see it struggle in less than perfect conditions and remain a more compact plant. A hardy biennial up to 1.5m (60in).

E. marginata (snow on the mountain) Z10   North America
A tall, hardy annual, upright species with plain green leaves. Green floral heads with unusual white margins appear from August to October. Flower arrangers often use the cut stems. It prefers well-drained soil in full sun. Height up to 1m (39in). Best to sow seed under cover first before planting outside.

E. marginata 'Summer Icicle' Z11   Garden Origin
Upright stems with green leaves. The flowering time is in August and September. Floral leaves are liberally covered in white, giving it a pleasant streaky appearance. It is smaller than the typical form at 45cm (18in). Grow as a half hardy annual.

E. x martinii AGM Z7   France
A natural hybrid between the species *E. characias* and *E. amygdaloides*. Rich green evergreen leaves, tinged purple, clothe deep red stems. Light green flowers with dark red nectar glands appear from April to July. It may repeat flower in October. Suffers from mildew and will become woody at the base with age. Ordinary soil in sun or part shade. A justifiably popular clump-forming perennial for the front half of the border. Height up to 80cm (32in).

E. x martinii 'Red Dwarf'   Garden Origin
Introduced by Janet and Richard Blenkinship of Orchard Nursery, Foston. Rich green evergreen leaves with a dark purple hue. The young new growth is red-tipped. Green flowers with red centres from March to June; may repeat flower in October. Suffers from mildew. Ordinary soil in sun or part shade. A dwarf clump-forming perennial. 30cm (1ft).

E. mellifera (honey spurge) Z9   Canary Islands
The flowers of this species are pale buff-yellow and richly honey-scented, appearing from April to June. It exhibits handsome, large, light green, evergreen foliage with a paler midrib and faint maroon

edges. It needs a well-drained soil and a sheltered site with some winter protection to establish itself, survive and flower. It will normally reach about 1.1m (40in) but if conditions are sheltered and favourable, can make a 2.5m (8ft) shrub. Propagate from seed, although cuttings are relatively easy in July. An odd seedling here and there may appear in the garden. Cut off dying flower stems in late summer and in early spring prune out any stems that have died back. A moderately hardy evergreen perennial shrub.

E. myrsinites AGM Z6 — Mediterranean

Thick prostrate stems with waxed blue-grey evergreen leaves. Lime-green flowers turn yellow from March to May. It needs a hot sunny position with well-drained soil. The leaves and stems will rot if they are in contact with wet soils for any length of time so it is best grown in a scree bed with a gravel mulch or at the edge of a dry stone wall or in a container. Propagation is easy from seed. A perennial with a central crown. 20cm (8in).

E. nereidum Z10 — Morocco

A clump-forming large, branching, leafy perennial. It is tall, up to 1.6m (5+ft) and may need staking. Coming from a warm climate it may be only moderately hardy. It requires a good moisture-retentive but well-drained garden soil in a sheltered position and with some additional winter protection to be happy. It is one of the last euphorbias to flower, providing a strong lime-yellow influence in the garden from August to October. Propagate from seed or cuttings.

E. nicaeensis (Nice spurge) Z7 — Balkans/Mediterranean

A very variable species with differences in height, flowering time, habit, leaf shape and colour. This has resulted in a large number of subspecies and forms. Described here are the ones which gardeners can acquire. Subspecies can be propagated from seed or cuttings. Cultivars need to be propagated from cuttings, taken in June and July. All require normal to well-drained garden soil in a sunny sheltered position. They are all well-behaved clump-forming perennials.

E. nicaeensis subsp. *nicaeensis* — Southern Europe

The most commonly available. In general, pink stems carry densely packed blue-grey evergreen foliage. The lime-yellow flowers contrast beautifully against the leaves from July to August. Upright stems with a variable height up to 90cm (30in) but often smaller.

E. nicaeensis subsp. *glareosa* — Central Europe

A subspecies, upright or procumbent according to the variety, with leaves slightly less blue and more spaced out on the stem. The usual lime-yellow flowers appear from July to September. 6-50cm (3 -20in).

E. nicaeensis subsp. glareosa var. glareosa
Numerous dull-pink, procumbent stems hug the ground all winter and into spring. It has grey-green pointed evergreen foliage. The stems only rear their heads to give their yellow floral display in August and September. It only reaches to 20cm (8in) high and is one of the last euphorbias to come into flower.

E. nicaeensis subsp. glareosa var. lasiocarpa
Bears a few erect stems 20-50cm (8-20in) high.

E. nicaeensis 'Abbey Dore'   Garden Origin
A seedling found at Abbey Dore Court garden in Herefordshire. It has semi-prostrate pink stems that contain leaves with a greener hue than the species. A mass of strong yellow floral heads is produced on a dome-shaped plant from July to September. 50cm (20in).

E. oblongata Z7   Eastern Mediterranean
Large lime-green flower heads in April and May. It has mid-green leaves on annual stems that are susceptible to mildew after the plant has flowered. Any soil in sun or part shade. Propagate from seed or cuttings. A clump-forming perennial up to 80cm (32in) for the middle of the border.

E. palustris (swamp spurge) AGM Z6   Central Europe
A vigorous leafy spurge with branching yellow heads from April to June. Annual mid-green leaves turn creamy yellow in autumn. It prefers moist soil but will cope with ordinary soil in sun or part shade. The stems are quite strong but will branch outwards making a very wide-open plant later in the season. It needs staking to keep it in bounds and stop it dominating surrounding plants. May suffer slightly from mildew. A large clump-forming perennial suitable for the middle or back of the border. Can be propagated by division, or cuttings root easily. 1.50m (5ft).

E. palustris 'Walenburg's Glorie'   Garden Origin
A selected form introduced by Michael Wickenden of Cally Gardens, Scotland. A clump-forming perennial very similar to, but more refined than, the species. It does not produce quite such a large plant. 1.2m (40in).

E. x paradoxa Z7   Eastern Europe
A natural hybrid between the species E. esula and E. salicifolia. Many narrow green, annual leaves clothe thin wiry stems that may need

staking. Yellow flowers from April to July. Any soil in sun or part shade. A vigorous runner and best grown in a container. 75cm (30in).

E. paralias (sea spurge) Z10   Europe/Middle East
A British native, growing on beaches and sand dunes around Europe. The sea spurge needs a sandy soil and some winter protection. Small pale blue-grey evergreen leaves are topped with small yellow flowers from June to September. A slightly tender clump-forming perennial. Propagate from seed. Up to 60cm (2ft).

E. pekinensis (Peking spurge) Z5   Mongolia/China
Bright pink stems with dark-green downy annual leaves that have a slightly grey appearance. In the autumn the leaves become a fiery red before falling. Well-branched yellow floral heads are produced in June and July. An unusual spurge to look at and quite rare. It needs good garden soil and a sunny aspect. Up to 60cm (2ft).

E. pilosa (hairy spurge) Z7   Asia
Mid-green annual leaves and yellow flowers in the summer. Normal garden soil in sun or part shade. Related to *E. cornigera* but not to *E. polychroma*. *E. pilosa* 'Major' is an incorrect name and plants with this name are *E. polychroma* Major'.

E. pithyusa (Balearic Islands spurge) Z9   N. Africa/S. Europe
Small, closely packed pointed glaucous evergreen leaves. Many branching stems, some of which do not flower. Those stems that do flower have small, mustard-coloured floral heads from July to October. It needs a well-drained soil in a warm sheltered position. Useful in a scree bed or a large rockery. Tends to become woody and straggly with age and best replaced every few years. Easily propagated from seed. 60cm (2ft). This is the most commonly available form of *pithyusa*.

E. pithyusa subsp. *cupanii*
Grey-green leaves clothe stems that have no non-flowering branches. Small clusters of yellow floral heads appear in May and June. It has a spreading rootstock and is best propagated from division. 50cm (20in).

E. polychroma AGM Z5   Central Europe
There is considerable debate on the naming of this species with some writers and nurseries using the name originally given by Linnaeus i.e. *E. epithymoides*. What is not in doubt is that this is a wonderful border perennial with a long list of virtues. It is fully hardy, doesn't seed or run, and makes a neat and compact clump with no staking required. It will tolerate most garden soils and will cope with sun or light shade.

Between March and May the plant will completely cover itself in a floral display of strong acid yellow. This luminous dome, up to 60cm (2ft) high and more across, is a stunning sight in spring. Brilliant in sunshine, in a shady bed it will illuminate its surroundings. It will send up a fresh set of shoots in summer and some cultivars will give a small second flush of flowers in September and October. Propagation of the species is easiest from division but seed and cuttings are also successful. Cultivars need to be propagated by careful division with a sharp knife in late winter, or cuttings in July. Its only drawback is a slight tendency to suffer from mildew after flowering. By this time, it is hardly noticeable, as the whole plant has faded into the background. The second flush of flowers and leaf does not generally have mildew. All varieties need to be cut back in late November when next year's growth buds will already have formed and be visible. It needs to be placed at the front of the border to show off its attributes and be fully appreciated.

E. polychroma 'Candy' (syn. E. p. 'Purpurea')   Garden Origin
Young annual foliage is a rich purplish-brown, fading to green later in the season. Orange-yellow flowers appear in April and May. Suffers with mildew. Any soil in sun or part shade. A clump-forming perennial 60cm (2ft).

E. polychroma 'Emerald Jade'   Garden Origin
A rare form and more refined cultivar with smaller stems and leaves. It grows 50cm (20in) tall and has chrome yellow flowers from March to May. It will give a good second flush in the autumn with attractive autumnal leaf colouring of pink, red and pale yellow.

E. polychroma 'Lacy' (syn. E. p. 'Variegata')   Garden Origin
An unusual variegated form, having leaves with light green centres and cream edges. The leaves can be quite wavy and young leaves have a fine pink hue to the edges. The flowers are a paler yellow than the species but appear at the same time. It is smaller and not as robust as the species, preferring sunshine to help the variegation. Any stems bearing plain green leaves must be removed immediately. 50cm (20in).

E. polychroma 'Major' AGM
Probably a selected wild form; the name is misleading, as this cultivar is slightly smaller than the species. The leaves are darker and the floral leaves are a paler yellow and usually come a little earlier. It may produce a second flush of flowers, and leaves turn crimson in the autumn. 50cm (20in).

E. polychroma 'Midas'

Originated at The Plantsmen (Jim Archibald and Eric Smith). A superb cultivar but not easy to find. Green, elongated leaves on annual stems bear a slight purple tint but not so much as in *E.p.* 'Candy'. The stems are stronger and sturdier, giving it a more upright habit and making it the tallest cultivar. Brilliant, eye-catching yellow floral heads cover the plant in April and May and it may repeat flower in the autumn. 80cm (30in). Grow as near to the front of the border as space will allow.

E. polychroma 'Orange Flush'   Garden Origin

The foliage is slightly darker than normal but its chief claim to fame is as, its name suggests, a strong deep orange flush to its floral leaves which persists throughout the flowering period. An attractive but rare cultivar selected by Jennifer Hewitt of Cleeton St Mary. 50cm (20in).

E. polychroma 'Sonnengold'   Garden Origin

This variety originated in Germany. The stems are pale pink and thin, often not being strong enough to support the mass of leaves and flowers, thus it has a slightly floppy untidy habit. The leaves have a pinky-purple tint and are very downy, making the taking of cuttings difficult as they hold the moisture and rot easily. The floral display is from March to May, with a second flush in the autumn. 50cm (20in).

E. portlandica (Portland spurge) Z8   Western Europe

A British native. Numerous small, pale green evergreen leaves clothe many thin pink stems coming from a central crown. Small yellow flowers from April to June. It needs a well-drained light soil in an open aspect. It usually produces bright red stems and leaves in the autumn. May seed around gently. A short-lived perennial 45cm (18in).

E. x pseudovirgata Z7   Austria

A cross between *E. esula* and *E. virgata*. Small mid-green, semi-evergreen leaves on lax stems that will need supporting. Tiny yellow/green floral heads appear from May to August. It suffers from mildew. Ordinary soil in sun or part shade. A running perennial, best suited for a wild garden. 1m (39in).

E. 'Purple Preference' Z7   Garden Origin

A plant introduced by Jenny and Tim Fuller from Norfolk; it is best described as a tall form of *E. amygdaloides* 'Purpurea'. Excellent foliage colour in autumn and winter but the stems are weak and cannot support the yellow flowers in spring, necessitating a lot of staking. It also suffers badly from mildew. 1m (39in).

E. Redwing = E. 'Charam' Z7   Garden Origin
A new compact evergreen cultivar introduced by Bernard Tickner of
Fullers Mill, West Stow. Purplish-green leaves are topped in late
winter with tight floral heads that turn increasingly red. They then
open up into large pale yellow *characias*-like floral heads that cover the
plant from March to May. Needs a well-drained loam in sun and half
shade. It is disease free and will reach 50cm (20in).

E. rigida Z9   Mediterranean
An unusual spurge, it needs a well-drained stony soil and a warm
sheltered position and makes a first rate scree garden or large rockery
plant. It has upwardly arching stems carrying sharply-pointed pale
grey succulent-like leaves. It may sometimes be shy to flower but
when it does, yellow flowers are produced from February to April
Propagate from seed. 60cm (2ft).

E. rigida 'Sardis'   Turkey
Collected in Turkey by Chris Brickell. Thick fleshy stems have steely,
blue-grey, pointed leaves with purple edges deepening in colour in the
winter. Rich, custard-yellow flowers develop from February to April.
The plant is more prostrate than the typical form. A superb plant that
needs to be grown where it can be viewed at close quarters; it doesn't
look out of place in a container Propagate from seed. 30cm (1ft).

E. sarawschanica (Zeravshan spurge) Z6   Central Asia
One of the leafy clump-forming spurges from Asia that are best grown
towards the back of the border. It has mid-green, droopy leaves on tall
lax stems, which give this plant a willowy appearance. Lime-yellow
floral heads are produced from May to July. It requires a good garden
soil in sun or part shade. Propagate from seed or cuttings. It makes a
tall plant at 1.50m (5ft) and may need staking.

E. schillingii (Schilling's spurge) AGM Z8   Himalaya
Handsome grey-green foliage, with deep red edges and a white mid
rib, is produced on annual upright pink stems. Clear yellow flowers
top the plant from July to September. It requires normal soil in sun or
part shade. A striking clump-forming perennial for the middle of the
summer border. Propagate from seed. 90cm (3ft).

E. seguieriana (Seguier's spurge) Z9 Central Europe/Afghanistan
Small, evergreen, densely packed narrow leaves on long thin arching
stems. The leaves are a light green-grey colour. Yellow flowers from
June to August. It is not a robust species and needs a free draining dry
soil and some winter protection from cold and rain. A slightly tender

clump-forming perennial best grown in a sheltered scree bed.
Propagate from seed. 60cm (2ft).

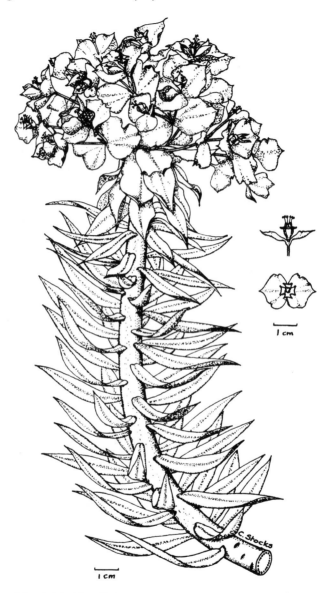

1 cm

1 cm

Euphorbia rigida '**Sardis**'

E. seguieriana subsp. *niciciana* Z8   Balkans/Asia Minor
Similar to the species but makes a better garden plant as it has a tougher constitution and a better floral display. Masses of tiny yellow floral heads cover the plant from June to October, giving it a long season of interest. Small, narrow grey-green evergreen leaves are borne on lax arching stems. It needs a well-drained soil and a sheltered sunny aspect. An unusual clump-forming perennial, ideal for the front of the border where it will delight throughout the summer. 60cm (2ft).

E. sikkimensis (**Sikkim spurge**) Z7   Himalaya
Bright pink new annual leaves and stems are a cheerful sight as they emerge in winter. The leaves turn pale green with age but the mid rib maintains the distinctive bright pink colour throughout. Yellow floral heads make an appearance from June to August. It requires normal soil in sun or part shade. Can suffer from mildew later in the season making the stem leaves defoliate. It will run slowly making propagation by division the easiest option. A distinctive clump-forming perennial best suited to the back of the border. 1.15m (3¾ft).

E. soongarica (**Dzungaria spurge**) Z7   Central Asia
This will make a very large plant and needs to be given plenty of space at the back of the border. The tall, willowy, branching annual stems, up to 1.8m (6ft) support mid-green leaves. It will probably need staking. The floral display is yellow and lasts from July to September. It prefers a reasonably moisture-retentive soil in sun or light shade. A clump-forming perennial; can be propagated from seed, cuttings or division.

E. spinosa Z9   Mediterranean
A small shrub with many, very thin, branching stems which persist when dead making it feel quite spiny but it is not as fierce or as sharp as *E acanthothamnos*. It grows only to 30cm (1ft) high but can produce wide clumps, so is best used at the front of the border or in a large rock garden. A mass of tiny yellow and orange flowers is produced from May to August. Propagate from seed or cuttings and trim it back every spring.

E. stricta (**syn. *E.* 'Golden Foam'**) Z6   Europe
Many tiny yellow flowers on a multi-branched floral head cover this plant from May to August giving it a light frothy feel. Small mid-green leaves grow on pinkish, upright stems. Any garden soil with a sunny aspect. It has good autumn colour in its second year but will seed around prolifically if allowed. An unusual hardy biennial spurge for

the wild garden, up to 90cm (3ft).

E. stygiana Z9   Azores

Makes a 10m (39ft) tree in its native habitat, where it has become an endangered species. Thick branching stems produce large luxuriant, dark green evergreen leaves with a pale midrib. It needs a good, rich, well drained soil and winter protection to survive and even then may not flower reliably. With the correct conditions, pale yellow flowers are produced in May and June. Raise from seed or from cuttings taken at the end of June from thinner side shoots. A slightly tender thicket-forming perennial. It makes a wonderful garden perennial if grown well but is rare in cultivation. 90cm (3ft).

E. terracina (**Terracina spurge**) Z10   Mediterranean

This has greyish-blue evergreen leaves well spaced out on the stems and lime-yellow floral heads in June and July. It needs a well-drained sunny, sheltered position and even then is only marginally hardy. Propagate from seed. 60cm (2ft).

E. veneris Z10   Cyprus

Small, pointed glaucous evergreen leaves on prostrate stems. The first euphorbia of the year to flower with small yellow floral heads from January to March. Unique to Cyprus where it replaces *E. myrsinites*. It needs a warm sunny position in a stony, free-draining soil and even then it is only moderately hardy. 20cm (8in).

E. villosa Z7   Europe

A fairly large leafy clump-forming perennial suitable for the back half of the border. Annual stems carry grey-green foliage that turns a distinctive pinky-red colour in the autumn. The branching yellow floral heads are very attractive from April to June. It requires a normal soil in sun or part shade. Propagate from cuttings in July. 1.2m (4ft).

E. virgata Z7   Europe - Central Asia

Many slender stems with mid-green semi-evergreen leaves. Lime-yellow flowers occur from May to July. Any soil in sun or part shade. It will need staking later in the season to stop it sprawling and becoming untidy. A vigorous running perennial making propagation easy from division. It can grow up to 1m (39in) and is really only suitable for the wild garden.

E. wallichii (**Wallich's spurge**) Z9   Himalaya

Most plants listed under this name are incorrectly named and will probably be *E. cornigera*. This was the result of some incorrectly labelled imported seed. The main differences are that *E. wallichii*, at 40-65cm. (16-26in) is smaller than *E. cornigera*, and the yellow flowers appear earlier in May and June. Wallich's spurge is quite rare in cultivation and is a challenge to grow. It needs a slightly moist soil in a sunny spot to be happy. It is slow to establish and if it is not happy it will soon die. Stems, which have a slight red pigmentation, carry green annual foliage. Propagation is from seed or occasionally an odd runner may appear which can be detached and potted up.

Euphorbia seguierian **subsp.** *niciciana*

HARDINESS ZONES

Zone	Average Minimum Winter Temperature
5	-29 to -23°C
6	-23 to -18°C
7	-18 to -12° C
8	-12 to -7°C
9	-7 to -1° C
10	-1 to 4°C
11	above 4° C

Where to see Euphorbias

THERE ARE THREE NATIONAL COLLECTIONS of euphorbia, geographically well dispersed and with very differing garden environments. One is in a walled garden at Oxford Botanic Garden, one is in a nurseryman's exposed hilltop garden in Northern Ireland and one is on an allotment on the edge of the Pennines just outside Sheffield. Each of them has well over 100 euphorbias on view to the public.

1. Oxford Botanic Garden, Rose Lane, Oxford, OX1 4AZ. Euphorbias are all together and labelled in the Order Beds, which are inside the walled garden part of the garden. Open all year. Contact Timothy Walker 01865 276920

2. Ballyrogan Nurseries, The Grange, Ballyrogan, Newtownards, N. Ireland, BT23 4SD. The euphorbias are spread throughout this 3-acre garden containing many hundreds of other plants and two more National Collections. Open by appointment. Contact Gary Dunlop 01247 810451.

3. c/o 26 Casson Drive, Harthill, Sheffield, S26 7WA. The euphorbias are labelled and contained in twelve island beds of mixed herbaceous planting. Open by appointment or there is an annual Open Day at the beginning of May. Contact Don Witton 01909 771366.

Other gardens where a good number of euphorbias will be found are listed below.

Abbey Dore Court Garden, Abbey Dore, Herefordshire.
Arley Hall Garden, Northwich, Cheshire.
The Beth Chatto Gardens, Elmstead Market, Colchester, Essex.
Binney Plants, Broxbourn, Edinburgh, Scotland.
Cally Gardens, Gatehouse of Fleet, Castle Douglas, Scotland.
Cambridge Botanic Garden, Cambridge.
Catforth Gardens, Catforth, Preston, Lancashire.
The Dell Garden, Bressingham, Diss, Norfolk.
Holehird Garden, Troutbeck, Windermere, Cumbria.
The River Garden, Sleights, Whitby, Yorkshire.
Roger Turner's garden, 7 All Saints Villas Road, Cheltenham.
The Royal Botanical Gardens, Kew, Richmond, London.
The Royal Horticultural Society Garden, Wisley, Woking, Surrey.
Sir Harold Hillier Garden and Arboretum, Romsey, Hampshire.

Where to buy Euphorbias

THE RHS PLANT FINDER lists many nurseries up and down the country that stock and sell euphorbias. Many incorporate euphorbias as part of a general range of herbaceous perennials. Some nurseries may stock one or two of the harder-to-find euphorbias. These are worth seeking out for a plant that is particularly wanted. There are, however, some nurseries that specialise in euphorbias and offer a greater number of plants in a wider range of varieties. For opening times and other details consult a current edition of *The RHS Plant Finder*.

England
Beth Chatto Nursery, Elmstead Market, Colchester, Essex.
Birkheads Cottage Garden Nursery, Sunniside, Newcastle upon Tyne.
Cotswold Garden Flowers, Badsey Evesham, Worcestershire.
Firvale Perennials, 26 Casson Drive, Harthill, Sheffield.
Gardiner's Hall Plants, Braiseworth, Eye, Suffolk.
Mill Cottage Plants, Wookey, Somerset.
Monksilver Nursery, Cottenham, Cambridgeshire.
Pandora Nursery, Horndean, Waterlooville, Hampshire.
Perry's Plants, Sleights, Whitby, Yorkshire.

Ireland
Ballyrogan Nurseries, The Grange, Ballyrogan, Newtownards, Co. Down.

Scotland
Binney Plants, Binney Estate, Broxbourn, West Lothian.
Cally Gardens, Gatehouse of Fleet, Castle Douglas.

France
Les Jardins d'En Face, La Ville au Monnier, 35730, Pleurtuit.

Some helpful lists

Here are some self-explanatory tables which may influence the gardener to purchase (or not) plants for their particular garden style or tastes.

STARTER PACK OF 6

These plants, suitable for a complete beginner, would offer a broad sample of euphorbias with spring and summer flowers, deciduous and evergreen leaves, a variety of leaf shape and colour, tall and short habits and with red as well as yellow flowers. Easily obtainable, and trouble free.

E. amygdaloides var. *robbiae*
E. characias subsp. *characias* 'Humpty Dumpty'
E. griffithii 'Dixter'
E. myrsinites
E. polychroma
E. schillingii

DISEASE RESISTANT PACK OF 6

These are the best species - in the author's garden - for avoiding mildew or rust. They are disease-free throughout the year.

E. ceratocarpa
E. donii
E. myrsinites
E. nicaeensis
E. pithyusa
E. rigida

CONTAINER PACK OF 6

Some euphorbias are quite happy in containers, pots or sinks (*E. myrsinites* has been used in hanging baskets). With others it is a good idea to keep them restricted in a container.

E. capitulata
E. cyparissias 'Fens Ruby'
E. cyparissias 'Orange Man'
E. myrsinites
E. paralias
E. rigida 'Sardis'

WINTER INTEREST TOP 6

Obviously all evergreen, the leaves add shape and colour to the winter scene in the garden. All will look good on New Year's Day.
Listed in order of the author's preference.

E. characias subsp. *wulfenii* 'Purple and Gold'
E. characias subsp. *characias* 'Perry's Winter Blusher'
E. rigida 'Sardis'
E. nicaeensis
E. characias subsp. *wulfenii* 'Emmer Green'
E. amygdaloides 'Purpurea'

SUMMER FLOWERS TOP 6

All these plants produce their blooms well after the peak flowering time of April and May. They display the luminous acid euphorbia yellow some time between June and September.
Listed in order of the author's preference.

E. donii
E. jacquemontii
E. seguieriana subsp. *niciciana*
E. sikkimensis
E. nereidum
E. schillingii

A PERSONAL FAVOURITE DOZEN

The all-time favourites of the author. Listed in order of preference. However, there are plenty of other excellent euphorbias not on this list.

E. polychroma 'Midas'
E. griffithii 'King's Caple'
E. donii
E. characias subsp. *wulfenii* 'Purple and Gold'
E. rigida 'Sardis'
E. griffithii 'Dixter'
E. characias 'Portuguese Velvet'
E. nicaeensis
E. jacquemontii
E. mellifera
E. seguieriana subsp. *niciciana*
E. characias 'Emmer Green'

Having eulogised over many excellent euphorbias and their garden uses, I feel that it is only fair to write two more lists of euphorbias with lesser virtues. (Some would call them faults.) Readers may wish to avoid them or regard them as a challenge. Despite their faults, I think that they still deserve a place in the garden - but there again, I'm slightly biased.

TOP 6 SEEDERS.

These are all either biennials or short lived perennials and in order to ensure their own survival produce an abundance of seed. *E. peplus* is a weed and is not included.

E. stricta
E. lathyris
E. helioscopia
E. hyberna
E. corallioides
E. dulcis 'Chameleon'

TOP 6 RUNNERS.

The roots do most of their running in winter and can travel a metre or more depending on the soil. *E.a.* var. *robbiae* and *E. griffithii* are both "walkers" for the author.

E. x *paradoxa*
E. virgata (and *E. pseudovirgata*)
E. esula
E. cyparissias (and cultivars)
E. amygdaloides var. *robbiae*
E. griffithii

Appendix: the euphorbia year

MONTH	• GARDEN TASKS	EUPHORBIAS IN FLOWER
January	• Carefully knock any freshly fallen snow off evergreen species.	*hyberna, veneris*
February	• Divide and pot up running species: e.g. *cyparissias, esula, griffithii, robbiae, virgata.* • Plant out new plants in favourable conditions.	'Humpty Dumpty', 'John Tomlinson', 'Purple and Gold', 'Perry's Winter Blusher', *corallioides, hyberna,* x *martinii, rigida, rigida* 'Sardis', *veneris.*
March	• Early in the month dig up and transplant euphorbias that are to be moved. • Plant out new plants • Sow seeds outdoors under glass. • Fork over ground around established plants; remove weeds; mulch. • Apply a general-purpose fertilizer. • Continue to divide running species.	*capitulata, cyparissias* & cvs., *corallioides,* 'Chameleon', *hyberna,* x *martinii, myrsinites,* 'Purple Preference', Redwing, *rigida, rigida* 'Sardis', *robbiae, veneris.*
April	• Last chance to divide runners • Pot on rooted cuttings that have over-wintered under glass. • Prick out seedlings from March sowing. • Watch for greenfly on young shoots and plants of *E. characias*; remove by hand or spray if there is a large number.	*amygdaloides* & cvs, *capitulata, characias* & cvs., *corallioides, cyparissias* & cvs., *donii, dulcis, dulcis* 'Chameleon', *hyberna,* x *martinii, mellifera, myrsinites, palustris, polychroma* & cvs., *portlandica,* 'Purple Preference', Redwing, *rigida, villosa.*

53

Month	Tasks	In flower
May	• Take cuttings of E. characias. • Enjoy the spectacular spring display of euphorbias at their peak. • Erect stakes around esula, x martinii, palustris, paradoxa, pseudovirgata, 'Purple Preference', villosa and virgata before they get too big.	altissima, amygdaloides & cvs, brittingeri, capitulata, ceratocarpa, characias & cvs., cyparissias & cvs., donii, dulcis, dulcis 'Chameleon', esula, griffithii & cvs., jacquemontii, lathyris, x martinii, mellifera, myrsinites, nicaeensis, oblongata, palustris, paradoxa, polychroma & cvs., portlandica, 'Purple Preference', Redwing, sarawschanica, seguieriana, stricta, stygiana, villosa, virgata, wallichii.
June	• Collect seed of E. characias. • Keep the hoe busy on bare soil to kill any germinating weeds. • Take cuttings of capitulata, characias cvs., griffithii cvs., jacquemontii, x martinii, oblongata, palustris, pekinensis, 'Purple Preference'. Mildew can be a problem this month after some species have flowered; spray if necessary.	altissima, amygdaloides, barrelieri, brittingeri, ceratocarpa, cornigera, donii, esula, Excalibur, jacquemontii, mellifera, nicaeensis, palustris, paradoxa, paralias, portlandica, sarawschanica, schillingii, seguieriana, spinosa, stricta, stygiana, virgata, & pseudovirgata, wallichii.
July	• Remove all dead flower stems from spring flowering plants. • Take cuttings of cultivars of characias, griffithii and polychroma; also of 'Purple Preference', Excalibur, and species which are difficult from seed, e.g. capitulata, jacquemontii, pekinensis, seguieriana, sikkimensis, • Water newly planted plants if weather is dry. • Keep an eye out for mildew. • Keep hoe working between plants. • Pot up young plantlets from March seed sowing.	barrelieri, ceratocarpa, cognata, cornigera, Excalibur, jacquemontii, nicaeensis & subspecies, paralias, pekinensis, pithyusa, pseudovirgata, sarawschanica, schillingii, seguieriana & subsp. niciciana, sikkimensis, soongarica, spinosa, stricta.

August	• Trim back and tidy up any untidy growth. • Pot up all rooted cuttings. • Start collecting all available seed when ripe. • Put seed heads in a paper bag and label. • Continue to weed if necessary.	*ceratocarpa, cognata, corallioides, cornigera, nereidum, nicaeensis* & subspecies, *parallas, pekinensis, pithyusa, pseudovirgata, schillingii, seguieriana,* & subsp. *niciciana, sikkimensis, soongarica, spinosa.*
September	• Continue potting up rooted cuttings. • Continue collecting seed. • Dead-head and dig up biennial species (*lathyris, stricta*) before they seed around. • Move up into pots one size larger those plants potted up in July.	*ceratocarpa, cognata, nereidum, pekinensis, pithyusa, schillingii, seguieriana* & subsp. *niciciana, spinosa.* 2nd flush: 'Lambrook Yellow', 'Perry's Tangerine', 'Perry's Winter Blusher', *corallioides, polychroma* cultivars, x *martinii.*
October	• Prepare ground for new plants by digging deeply and incorporating plenty of grit or humus. • Complete harvesting seed. • Remove all stakes and cut back all clump-forming plants to ground level when they have died down.	*nereidum, pithyusa, schillingii, seguieriana,* & subsp. *niciciana.* 2nd flush: *amygdaloides* 'Purpurea', *ceratocarpa, characias,* 'Perry's Tangerine', 'Perry's Winter Blusher', *corallioides, polychroma* cultivars, x *martinii.*
November	• Move potted up cuttings and seedlings under glass for the winter. • Finish cutting back all deciduous plants • In mild, dry weather dig up and divide mature clumps which have outgrown their space.	*ceratocarpa, characias, hyberna,* x *martinii.*
December	• Dead head any second-flush flowers. • Protect less hardy species in very cold weather. • Enjoy the winter show of evergreen leaves.	*hyberna, ceratocarpa*

References

Bird, R. *The Complete Book of Hardy Perennials.* Ward Lock, 1993

Bird, R. *The Cultivation of Hardy Perennials.* Batsford, 1994

Brickell, C. (ed.) *The RHS A-Z Encyclopaedia of Garden Plants.* Dorling Kindersley, 1996

Dunlop, G. 'Three Cultivars and a Throwback' in *The Hardy Plant Vol. 21 No. 1,* 1999

Gledhill, D. *The Names of Plants.* Cambridge University Press, 1996

Hay, R. & Beckett, K. *The Readers Digest Encyclopaedia of Plants and Flowers.* Hodder & Stoughton, 1971

Lord, T. (ed.) *The RHS Plant Finder.* Dorling Kindersley, 1999

Phillips, R. & Rix, E. M. *Perennials* Vols 1 & 2. Macmillan, 1993

Tickner, B. '*Euphorbia* Redwing' in *The Hardy Plant* Vol. 20 No. 2, 1998

Turner, R. *Euphorbias: A Gardeners' Guide* Batsford 1995

Wilford, R. 'Rock Garden Spurges' in *The Bulletin of the Alpine Garden Society,* Vol. 67. 1999